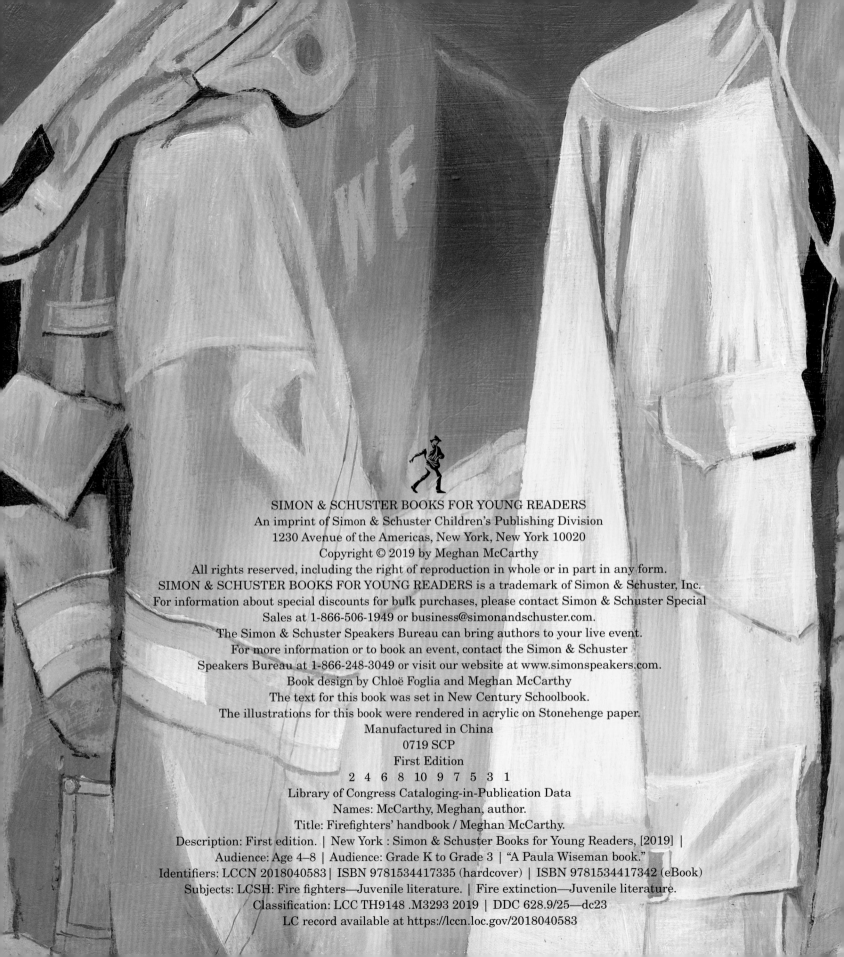

SIMON & SCHUSTER BOOKS FOR YOUNG READERS
An imprint of Simon & Schuster Children's Publishing Division
1230 Avenue of the Americas, New York, New York 10020
Copyright © 2019 by Meghan McCarthy
All rights reserved, including the right of reproduction in whole or in part in any form.
SIMON & SCHUSTER BOOKS FOR YOUNG READERS is a trademark of Simon & Schuster, Inc.
For information about special discounts for bulk purchases, please contact Simon & Schuster Special
Sales at 1-866-506-1949 or business@simonandschuster.com.
The Simon & Schuster Speakers Bureau can bring authors to your live event.
For more information or to book an event, contact the Simon & Schuster
Speakers Bureau at 1-866-248-3049 or visit our website at www.simonspeakers.com.
Book design by Chloë Foglia and Meghan McCarthy
The text for this book was set in New Century Schoolbook.
The illustrations for this book were rendered in acrylic on Stonehenge paper.
Manufactured in China
0719 SCP
First Edition
2 4 6 8 10 9 7 5 3 1
Library of Congress Cataloging-in-Publication Data
Names: McCarthy, Meghan, author.
Title: Firefighters' handbook / Meghan McCarthy.
Description: First edition. | New York : Simon & Schuster Books for Young Readers, [2019] |
Audience: Age 4–8 | Audience: Grade K to Grade 3 | "A Paula Wiseman book."
Identifiers: LCCN 2018040583| ISBN 9781534417335 (hardcover) | ISBN 9781534417342 (eBook)
Subjects: LCSH: Fire fighters—Juvenile literature. | Fire extinction—Juvenile literature.
Classification: LCC TH9148 .M3293 2019 | DDC 628.9/25—dc23
LC record available at https://lccn.loc.gov/2018040583

Firefighters' Handbook

Meghan McCarthy

A Paula Wiseman Book
Simon & Schuster Books for Young Readers
New York   London   Toronto   Sydney   New Delhi

Welcome! Soon you will learn everything you need to know to become a firefighter. The training is hard, but the job is harder, so be prepared!

You will have to pass some tough tests to become a firefighter. One test is called the Candidate Physical Ability Test (CPAT). To prepare for the test, try . . .

pull-ups

running

push-ups

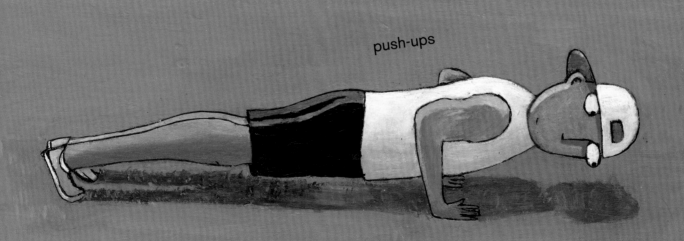

bike riding

walking

squats or
climbing stairs

It's time for the CPAT! Here are some of the tests you will need to pass.

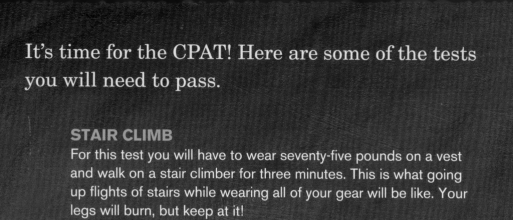

STAIR CLIMB

For this test you will have to wear seventy-five pounds on a vest and walk on a stair climber for three minutes. This is what going up flights of stairs while wearing all of your gear will be like. Your legs will burn, but keep at it!

(For the rest of the tests you will be wearing fifty pounds attached to a vest.)

HOSE DRAG

You must drag a hose around an obstacle. You will walk 100 feet, which is about the length of a basketball court.

EQUIPMENT CARRY

Next grab two heavy saws and carry them seventy-five feet. This will test muscles in your arms, hands, and legs. Firefighters need to be strong!

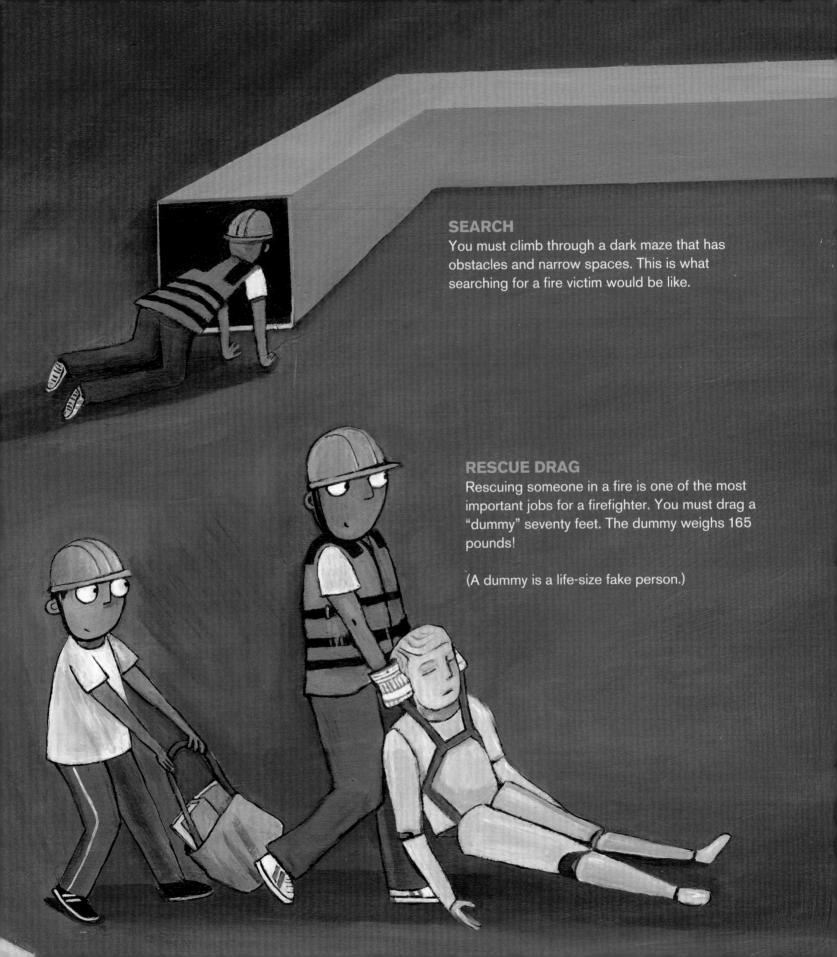

SEARCH
You must climb through a dark maze that has obstacles and narrow spaces. This is what searching for a fire victim would be like.

RESCUE DRAG
Rescuing someone in a fire is one of the most important jobs for a firefighter. You must drag a "dummy" seventy feet. The dummy weighs 165 pounds!

(A dummy is a life-size fake person.)

Being a firefighter isn't just a physical job. It's mental, too. Math, science, memory, and spatial reasoning are important.

Here's an example: Study this picture carefully and memorize as much of it as possible. At the end of the book you'll be asked questions about what you remember. Don't forget!

Firefighters are team players. Being helpful, learning to share, and getting along are all important traits for a firefighter to have. It is also important to have a good sense of right and wrong. Before becoming a firefighter, you must be interviewed.

What is the best way to handle a situation where your fellow firefighter often eats your cereal without asking? Do you:*

A) yell at him?
B) get even by eating his cereal?
C) report him to your superior?
D) talk to him to resolve the situation before reporting?

*Answer in the back of the book.

Congratulatons, you've made it into the academy. Now you are a "probie," which is short for "probationary firefighter." Becoming a probie means the real learning begins.

This is what you will wear. It's called Personal Protective Equipment or PPE for short. All of it together weighs about forty-five pounds!

helmet
Protects heads from falling objects. The helmets come in different colors depending on rank. The number helps identify the firefighter.

SCBA facepiece
This seals the face and prevents smoky air from being breathed. It is high-heat-and-flame resistant. SCBA stands for self-contained breathing apparatus.

SCBA regulator
This reduces pressure from the air cylinder.

SCBA air cylinder
This tank holds the air used to breathe in smoky conditions. This is sometimes called the "bottle" and is worn on the firefighter's back.

voice amplifier
Helps firefighters hear one another. Newer models are on the shoulder.

flashlight
This one is at a right angle so that it can be hung on the jacket. Firefighters carry other kinds of flashlights as well.

control module
Shows air pressure and air remaining. Also includes a personal alert safety system (PASS). The red emergency button sounds an alarm when pressed. It also goes off if it does not detect motion or in new models when a fall is detected.

kneepads
Used to protect knees when crawling.

reflective stripes
Used to make the firefighter more visible.

waist strap
This is part of the harness used for securing the SCBA air cylinder.

gloves
Used to protect hands from hot objects and other hazards.

turnout gear (sometimes called bunker gear)
This is what firefighters call their pants and jacket. The fabric is flame, heat, and water resistant, and inner layers wick water away from the body. The gear can be in different colors, mostly black or different shades of tan, though forest firefighters generally wear yellow. Why do some departments wear black and others tan? Tradition!

boots
They are fire, water, and puncture resistant.

Here are some of the tools you will use:

personal escape kit
Includes a D ring carabiner and rope. Used to escape from high structures.

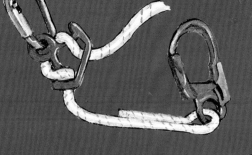

thermal imaging camera (TIC)
Used to show areas of heat in dark and smoke-filled environments where it is hard to see or through walls and doors.

sledgehammer
A striking tool used for breaking down doors and walls.

chain saw
Used mostly for ventilation, such as cutting holes in a roof to let out smoke and heat, and in the Forest Service for clearing trees.

wooden door chock
Used to prop open doors.

pick-head ax
A cutting and prying tool. Another ax firefighters use is the flat-head ax, which is both a striking and a cutting tool. When carried together with the Halligan bar, they are sometimes called "the irons."

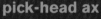

Halligan bar
Multipurpose tool comprising three parts: the claw, duckbill, and pike. Can be used for prying and breaking doors and locks, as an anchor to escape out of windows, to hold car hoods open, to break glass, to turn off gas meter valves, and much more.

wire cutters
Used to escape from entangled wires.

You'll ride in either a fire truck or an engine. A fire truck is like a giant toolbox, carrying tools to break down doors, cut holes for ventilation, and much more. There are different kinds of trucks with different kinds of ladders, some made to reach the tops of very tall city buildings.

Fire engines carry water, pumps, and hoses to put out fires.

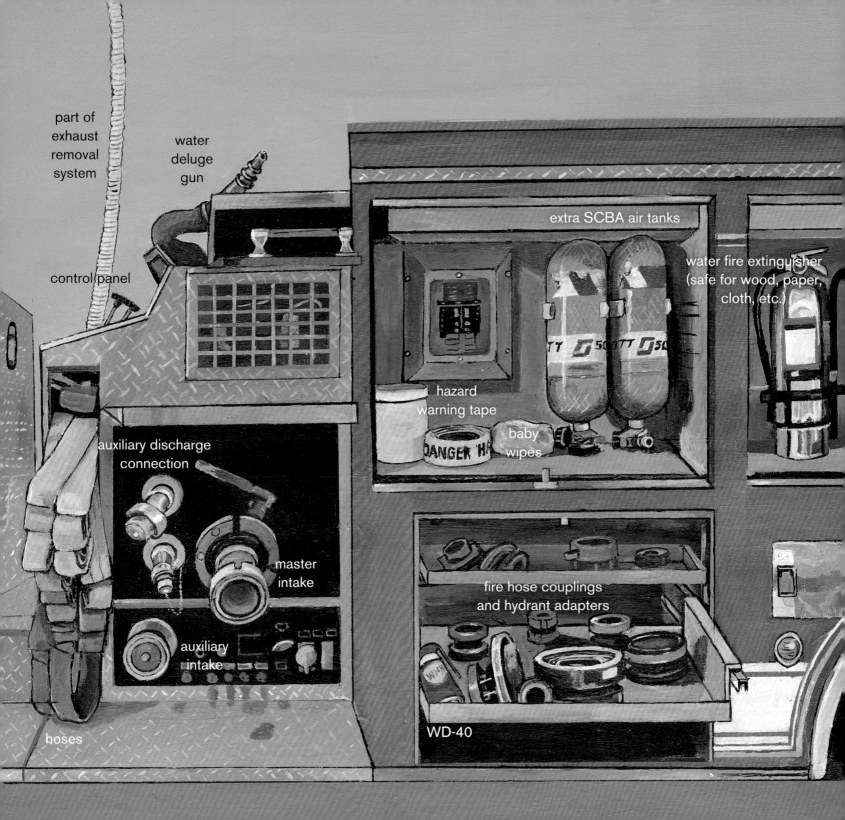

part of exhaust removal system

water deluge gun

control panel

extra SCBA air tanks

water fire extinguisher (safe for wood, paper, cloth, etc.)

hazard warning tape

baby wipes

auxiliary discharge connection

master intake

auxiliary intake

fire hose couplings and hydrant adapters

WD-40

hoses

Both engines and ladder trucks have many compartments.

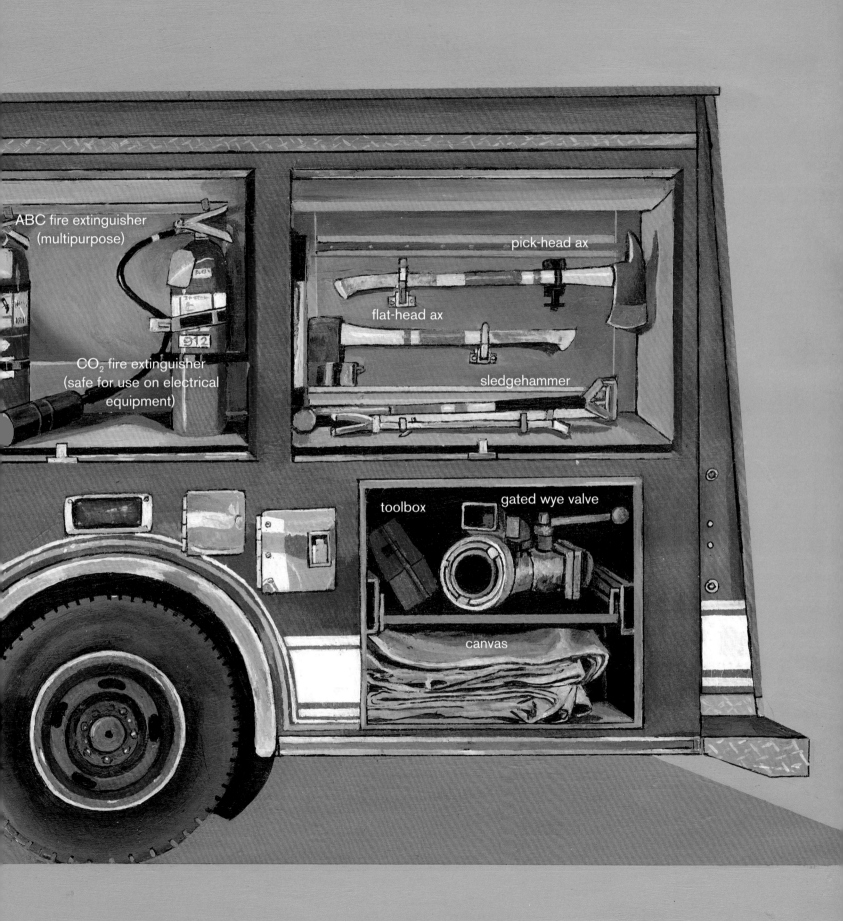

ABC fire extinguisher
(multipurpose)

pick-head ax

flat-head ax

CO_2 fire extinguisher
(safe for use on electrical
equipment)

sledgehammer

toolbox

gated wye valve

canvas

There are different places where
you can work as a firefighter that
you might not think of, such as on
the ocean . . .

at the airport . . .

You mustn't be afraid of heights.
Some truck ladders go very high!

You must also be comfortable going up and down ropes.

If you work for the Forest Service, you may have to rappel out of a helicopter.

You will train at something that looks like a movie set. Here you will practice putting out fires and saving dummies inside the buildings.

Be prepared to feel hot! When you go into some fire situations, temperatures can reach over one thousand degrees. Also be prepared for little visibility. Sometimes you can only see a foot's length in front of you.

Stay low to the ground, and crawl and feel your way along the walls.
You'll use your senses as a firefighter: sight, smell, touch, and hearing.
Always know your way out.

You may also need to be trained as a paramedic.
A paramedic responds to 911 medical calls . . .

gives CPR . . .

bandages wounds . . .

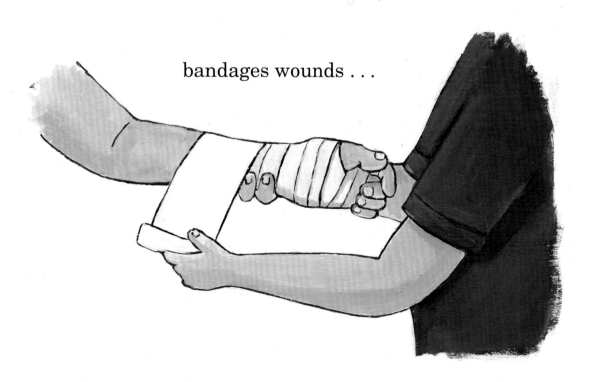

and stabilizes a
patient and gives
life support.

You will be the first line of defense when dealing
with sick or injured patients.

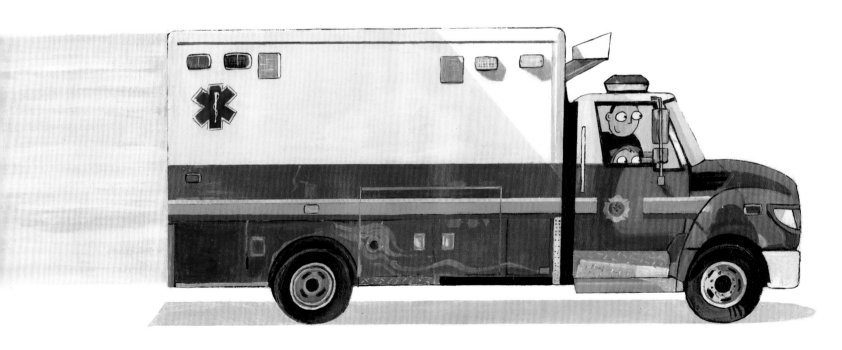

Once they are stabilized, they are rushed to the hospital,
where doctors will take over.

As a firefighter you may go on a lot of emergency calls, not all of them involving fire. A hydraulic tool named the Jaws of Life will pry and cut metal. Your training as a paramedic to help the injured will be useful.

Once you make it through the fire academy, you will be
assigned to a fire station.

You will likely work ten twenty-four-hour shifts per month.
That means you'll be spending a lot of time at the firehouse.

You will eat there . . .

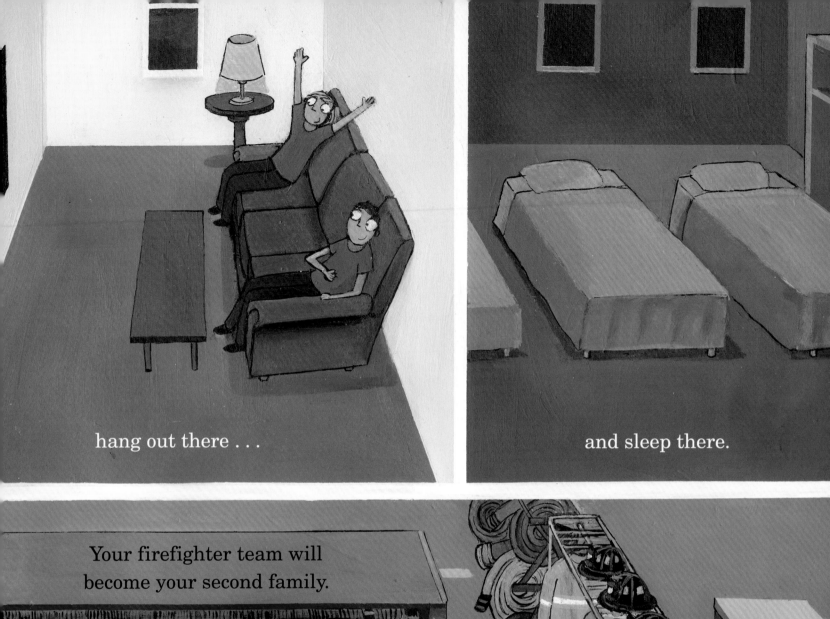

hang out there . . .

and sleep there.

Your firefighter team will become your second family.

There can be a lot of downtime, so you will also have chores:

cleaning dishes . . .

mopping floors . . .

and washing off the trucks.

After many hours of chores you
can sit back and relax.

But always be ready for a . . .

Fire!

Drop what you're doing . . .

slide down the pole . . .

put on your gear . . .

jump into the fire truck . . . and GO!

You are ready. You've trained for this and prepared well.
Now you can put out that fire and save lives.

As part of my research for the book, I talked to many firefighters. I asked Bob "Bubba" Parmenter, a retired Fire Department Battalion Chief in Warwick, Rhode Island, some questions and also asked some children for questions for Mr. Parmenter.

Why did you want to become a firefighter?
I became a volunteer firefighter at age fourteen at Hope-Jackson Fire Department in Hope, Rhode Island. My dad was a volunteer and back in those days there was not a lot of activity in the community, so me and most of my buddies got involved, and then I found I enjoyed the excitement of the job and the experience of helping others in our little town.

What were some memorable moments as a firefighter?
I have many moments that have stuck with me. I was involved in the fire service for almost fifty years. Unfortunately, my most memorable experience was the Station nightclub fire in West Warwick. One hundred people lost their lives that night and many were injured. I was on one of the first trucks to arrive, and that night remains vivid in my mind. On a lighter note, I have delivered a baby twice during my career—those are the rare happy moments that we get to be a part of. Most of the time we are called during the worst day of a person's life.

What is a battalion chief and what are the responsibilities?
A battalion chief is in charge of a platoon of firefighters. Warwick has a four-platoon system—we worked two ten-hour days, then two fourteen-hour nights, then four days off. I would work the same schedule. I had an office in one of the fire stations, and I slept in the station those two nights. On duty I was in charge of fifty-two on-duty firefighters. I would respond to any major call: fire, highway accident, marine incident, hazmat incidents, and any other run considered major. My job on these runs was to ensure that the incident ran smoothly. The safety of all firefighters is the number-one priority, and I was there as an incident commander.

Are there specific qualities you must possess to become a battalion chief?
To be a battalion chief you need to have good leadership skills and self-confidence. The lives of the firefighters could depend on a decision you make.

What was a typical day like as battalion chief or was there no typical day?
There never is a typical day in the fire service. We have a daily routine, but that often gets interrupted. When I first arrive on duty, I put my gear in the BC vehicle, make a quick check of my air-pack and all other gear, then get an update from the BC going off duty. The firefighters do the same: gear, equipment check, complete truck check, wash the truck. Then they have house duties to clean and maintain the station. Then they do some training—all this between runs to fire calls. Sometimes lunch never gets eaten.

When there's a house fire, what are the steps firefighters take to extinguish it?
Each company has an assignment depending on their dispatch order. The first arriving company gives a size-up of the situation over the radio—for example, "heavy fire showing"—and makes the initial attack with the driver operating the pump, and the officer and firefighter stretching the hose and attacking the fire.

Do you have any fire safety tips for children and their families?
The best thing for a family to do is to have smoke detectors, CO detectors, and an escape plan to make sure everyone gets out safely.

What were a few highlights of your career?
The highlights of my career were making the rank of BC, rescuing a five-year-old from a second-floor bedroom, assisting in two child-births, meeting George H. W. Bush when he was president, and the friendships and camaraderie that last till this day. It is a career like no other and words can't explain it. Those who have done the job understand: firefighters are always there for each other. And lastly, like I stated earlier, the Station fire, which was one of the most tragic fires in the United States.

Now that you've retired, what do you do with your time?
I stay in touch with many of the guys. A bunch of us golf once a week and we meet several times a year for dinner. I ski with a bunch of them, and a few of us hike together. Life is good.

• • • Children's Questions • • •

Mia: Why are fire trucks red?
There is no real reason for red fire trucks. Some are white, yellow, or lime green.

Mia: Do firemen really have a pole?
Most of the newer stations are built on one level and there is no need for a pole, but the poles are still found in the older fire stations.

Louis: Where do you get the water to put out the fires?
The water comes from a 500-gallon tank on the truck and fire hydrants on the street.

Soleil: What's the scariest fire you had to put out?
The scariest fire was when I and another firefighter fell into the basement through a hole that was in the floor and we had to be rescued out.

Sadie: Have you ever saved a baby from a fire?
I have never saved a baby but I did rescue a five-year-old girl.

Ruby: Has there ever been a fire that you couldn't put out?
We had a marina fire once and we couldn't get the fire out in one large boat, so we set it free to drift away from the dock.

Juliet: What do you like most about your job?
Being a firefighter is one of the most rewarding jobs you could have. Sometimes you get to make a difference for somebody that is having a real bad day. It's also very dangerous and not for everyone. But you build friendships and trust in each other because any day your life could depend on another firefighter. That's why we are so close and there is such a "brotherhood." But we do have women that are firefighters too.

Questions for the memory quiz found at the front of the book (crowd scene)

What instrument is the man playing?
What is the bird doing?
What kind of reptile is in the picture?
How many dogs are there?
What is the bright yellow symbol on the man's shirt?

• • •

Answer to the interview question found at the front of the book

D) Talk to him to resolve the situation before reporting.

• • •

Acknowledgments

Thanks to David Bettes, chief of the Oceanside, Long Island, Fire Department, for looking over my draft; to Rhode Island firefighter Mike Schmidt and retired chief Russ McCombs for answering random questions; to the firefighters at Engine 315 Ladder 125 in Queens, New York, for showing me around and letting me try on the heavy suit; to DJ McGouran of the Hope Valley-Wyoming, Rhode Island, Fire District for showing me the trucks in detail; and to Bubba for the wonderful Q&A!

• • •

Remembering Eli Blumberg—a joyful and kind boy who admired the brave work of firefighters and often dreamed about stepping into their boots, pants, jacket, and helmet one day!

• • •

Photo credits

"Bubba" Parmenter photo by Valerie Parmenter
Kids' photos courtesy of their families

• • •

Sources

Fire Engineering magazine: fireengineering.com
Firehouse magazine: firehouse.com
FireRescue magazine: firerescuemagazine.com
FireRescue1: firerescue1.com

For a complete bibliography, please go to meghan-mccarthy.com.